TABLE OF CONTENTS

Novel-Ties® are printed on recycled paper.

Copyright © 1982, 1993, 2018 by LEARNING LINKS

For the Teacher

This reproducible study guide consists of lessons to use in conjunction with the book *Bridge to Terabithia*. Written in chapter-by-chapter format, the guide contains a synopsis, pre-reading activities, vocabulary and comprehension exercises, as well as extension activities to be used as follow-up to the novel.

In a homogeneous classroom, whole class instruction with one title is appropriate. In a heterogeneous classroom, reading groups should be formed: each group works on a different novel at its reading level. Depending upon the length of time devoted to reading in the classroom, each novel, with its guide and accompanying lessons, may be completed in three to six weeks.

Begin using NOVEL-TIES for reading development by distributing the novel and a folder to each child. Distribute duplicated pages of the study guide for students to place in their folders. After examining the cover and glancing through the book, students can participate in several pre-reading activities. Vocabulary questions should be considered prior to reading a chapter; all other work should be done after the chapter has been read. Comprehension questions can be answered orally or in writing. The classroom teacher should determine the amount of work to be assigned, always keeping in mind that readers must be nurtured and that the ultimate goal is encouraging students' love of reading.

The benefits of using NOVEL-TIES are numerous. Students read good literature in the original, rather than in abridged or edited form. The good reading habits, formed by practice in focusing on interpretive comprehension and literary techniques, will be transferred to the books students read independently. Passive readers become active, avid readers.

SYNOPSIS

Jesse Oliver Aarons, Jr. is different. Not only is he the only boy in a family among four sisters, but he dares to enjoy sketching, which is hardly considered a masculine pursuit in the rural Virginia town of Lark Creek where he lives. His parents are too busy seeking out a living to pay much attention to him or provide him with any of life's luxuries.

Jess is a loner until Leslie Burke and her family move into the house next door. Even though Leslie is academically and athletically superior to Jess, and even though she is much more sophisticated than he, a strong bond of friendship develops between the two.

Jess and Leslie create their own private world in the woods across a creek. They build a castle and oversee their private kingdom which they call Terabithia. Their faithful subject, Leslie's puppy Prince Terrien, accompanies them there. They share their world of creative fantasy, using this secret place as a buffer against the outside world's injustices. Confident in each other's unwavering approval, Leslie reaches for new feats of bravery, while Jess becomes more self-assured and independent.

Their world is shattered unexpectedly on a wet spring day when Jess is a guest of his art teacher on a day trip to visit Washington's art museums. Leslie, bored with the tedium of a rainy day without Jess, decides to risk the swollen waters and strong current in order to cross the creek to Terabithia. Her attempt ends fatally, and Jess returns from his Washington excursion to discover that his closest friend is dead.

His grief passes through stages of negation, anger, sadness, and finally, resigned acceptance. Although Leslie has died, her impact upon Jess's growth is indelible. This is evident at the conclusion of the novel when Jess returns to Terabithia, independent and strong, able to bestow the title of Queen upon his favorite little sister May Belle.

PRE-READING ACTIVITIES

1. Preview the book by reading the title and author's name and by looking at the illustration on the cover. What do you think the book will be about? Where do you think it will take place? Have you read any other books by the same author?

2. Discuss with your classmates the qualities of a best friend. Should you and your best friend have the same interests and talents or should you and your best friend have opposite personalities? What responsibilities do you and your best friend have for each other? Should you and your best friend share everything or are there parts of your lives that should remain separate?

3. Imagine a place that would be your own private refuge. This would be somewhere away from the world of adults — a place where you could daydream, read, or just be by yourself. Draw a picture of what this ideal place would be like or find a picture in a newspaper or magazine to represent it. Then write a brief description of this place, telling why it would be special for you. As you read the book, compare your place to Terabithia.

4. Write a short piece of dialogue representing a conversation between you and a friend. Select a style of speech that either imitates the spoken language of average people you know, or a style of speech that imitates the style you imagine kings or queens would have spoken in the past. When writing dialect you should alter spelling to reflect the sound of spoken language. Then, as you read the book, observe how Katherine Paterson used dialect to reflect country speech and courtly speech.

5. At your school and among your friends, is there a double or a single standard for activities and personality traits that are considered acceptable for boys and girls? Would boys who like to draw, or dance, or cook, for example, be criticized? Can girls join athletic teams for all sports, or reveal intellectual ability without being teased? What are your feelings about traditional roles for boys and girls?

6. Have you ever had to face a personal tragedy involving the loss of someone you loved through abandonment, illness, or death? If so, how did you react to the tragedy? How did you express your grief? Did the event have any long-term effect on you?

7. Read the author's dedication at the beginning of the novel. Why do you think Katherine Paterson dedicated this book to her son? And why do you think he wanted Lisa's name on the dedication page, too?

8. Go to YouTube or try to find a recording of "Free to Be . . . You and Me." It can be found in a book of that title, written by Marlo Thomas. After you read the lyrics, try to guess why the words to this song have an important place in the novel you are about to read.

9. What are all the possible meanings of "bridge"? What might a bridge connect or bring together? Consider bridges that are physical structures and those that are not. As you read the book, think about all of the bridges you encounter.

CHAPTER 1: JESSE OLIVER AARONS, JR.

Vocabulary: Draw a line from each word on the left to its definition on the right. Then use the numbered words to fill in the blanks in the sentences below.

1. despised
2. stroll
3. crouched
4. brag
5. puny
6. obediently

a. stooped or bent low
b. respectfully; submissively
c. weak
d. walk leisurely
e. use boastful language
f. regarded with distaste or contempt

. . . .

1. It is better to _____ through the museum, looking at all the exhibits carefully, rather than racing through quickly.

2. A well-trained dog responds to its master _____ when it is called.

3. Even though he knew it was a healthy food, Jake _____ garlic because of its odor.

4. The runner _____ at the starting block, waiting for the race to begin.

5. After several weeks of good food and loving care, the formerly _____ puppy became strong and playful.

6. It is better to allow others to say good things about you than to _____ about yourself.

Language Study: These are examples of colloquial speech found in Chapter One. Translate each into standard speech.

1. Momma would be mad as flies in a jar.

   _____

2. He was the only boy smashed between two sisters on either side.

   _____

3. No one had more grit than he.

   _____

4. He won the whole shebang.

   _____

Chapter 1: Jesse Oliver Aarons, Jr. (cont.)

Background Information: In the first chapter the author conveys a great deal of background information. As you read, fill in as much of the following chart as possible.

Time of year the story begins: _____		
Location of Aaron farm: _____		
Members of Aaron family	Age	Occupation

> Read to Learn why Jess was troubled at home

Questions:

1. What family problems did Jess face?

2. What challenge did Jess take upon himself? What did this reveal about his personality?

3. Why wasn't Jess interested in the people moving into the house next door?

Questions for Discussion:

1. Have you ever taken on a challenge as great as the one Jess set for himself? If so, why did you challenge yourself in that way? Did you succeed?

2. Did the conversations among Jess and his sisters seem realistic to you? Did they remind you of anything that happens in your household?

3. Do you think Jess was treated fairly or unfairly by his mother and sisters?

Writing Activity:

Write about something you would like to accomplish. Tell why this would be important to you and how your life might be changed if you were to succeed. Also, describe ways you might achieve this goal.

CHAPTER 2: LESLIE BURKE

Vocabulary: Use the context to figure out the meaning of the underlined word in each of the following sentences. Then compare your definition with a dictionary definition.

1. Pandemonium broke loose in the auditorium when someone shouted "fire."

    Your definition   _____

    Dictionary definition _____

2. It was hypocritical of my sister to say she disliked my new tee shirt when she had already borrowed it twice.

    Your definition   _____

    Dictionary definition _____

3. My skin turned red and blistered when scalding tea was accidentally spilled on my hand.

    Your definition   _____

    Dictionary definition _____

4. The class cut out paper turkeys and planned a skit in anticipation of Thanksgiving.

    Your definition   _____

    Dictionary definition _____

5. It is easier to endure long walks in the snow if you are dressed in warm clothing and high boots.

    Your definition   _____

    Dictionary definition _____

> Read to learn about Jess's love of drawing.

Questions:

1. What did it mean that "Jess drew like some people drank whiskey"?
2. How did Jess's father feel about his son's drawing? Why did he feel that way?
3. Why was Jess so fond of Miss Edmunds?
4. Why didn't Jess respond to his new neighbor's offer of friendship?

Questions for Discussion:

1. Why do you think Jess liked to draw crazy animals with problems? What might this suggest about his personality?
2. Do you think Jess's father should have hugged his son? Do you think there is an age beyond which children should not receive their parents' physical signs of affection?

Chapter 2: Leslie Burke (cont.)

Literary Device: Simile

A simile is a figure of speech in which two unlike objects are compared using the words "like" or "as." For example:

> He [Jess] kept the knowledge of it [Miss Edmunds' admiration of his talent] buried inside himself like a pirate treasure.

What is being compared?

_____

Why is this better than saying, "He kept the knowledge secret"?

_____

_____

Literary Elements:

I. *Characterization* — The author introduced two new characters in this chapter. Indicate who they are and tell what you know about each one (appearance, personality traits, occupation, etc.)

Name: _____

_____

_____

Name: _____

_____

_____

II. *Setting* — Setting refers to the time and place where story events occur. How would you describe Lark Creek, its people, and the school Jess attended?

_____

_____

_____

_____

Writing Activity:

Write about something that you do that is not appreciated by others or write about some way in which you are the object of unfair treatment. Tell whether you react with sadness and acceptance as Jess did or do you react another way.

CHAPTER 3: THE FASTEST KID IN THE FIFTH GRADE

Vocabulary: Draw a line from each word on the left to its definition on the right. Then use the numbered words to fill in the blanks in the sentences below.

1. retreat   a. easily noticed; attracting special attention

2. focus   b. extended period of dry weather

3. gaze   c. concentrate one's thoughts

4. postponed   d. look steadily

5. repulsive   e. put off until later; deferred

6. drought   f. disgusting

7. conspicuous   g. withdraw

. . . .

1. Wearing an overcoat in July would make you _____ on the beach.

2. Because of his _____ table manners, no one would join him for lunch.

3. The baseball game was _____ because of heavy rain.

4. The month-long _____ caused crops to die on the vines.

5. You may damage your eyes if you _____ at the sun without the protection of dark glasses.

6. The runner was told to _____ his attention on the finish line.

7. The soldiers had to _____ in the face of stronger, better equipped opposing forces.

Word Study: Connotation

Connotation refers to the secondary meanings of a word or the ideas it suggests. For example, the words *skinny* and *slim* mean the same thing, but *skinny* has a bad connotation and *slim* has a good connotation. Here are three clusters of words with similar meanings. Discuss their different connotations.

softly spoken words	facial expression	to look at
mumble	smile	stare
mutter	grin	glare
whisper	smirk	gaze
		obseve

Chapter 3: The Fastest Kid in the Fifth Grade (cont.)

> Read to find out about Jess's new neighbor and classmate

Questions:

1. Why did Leslie make such a dramatic first impression on the fifth-grade class? How did Leslie to feel about their reaction to her?

2. Why was Jess unhappy about his first day in fifth grade?

3. Why did Jess say that he wanted Leslie to run in the boys' race?

Questions for Discussion:

1. Was there anything about Jess's school that revealed that the story took place in the 1970s and not today? In what ways was Jess's school different from your own?

2. What conflicting emotions did Jess have in this chapter towards Leslie? What caused him to feel this way?

Literary Device: Metaphor

A metaphor in literature is a figure of speech in which a comparison between two unlike objects is suggested or implied. For example:

> They were not supposed to talk during lunch, but it was the first day and even Monster-mouth Myers shot fewer flames on the first day.

What is Mrs. Myers being compared to?

_____

What does this comparison suggest about Mrs. Myers' character and the children's feelings about her?

_____

_____

Writing Activity:

What is your opinion of girls participating with boys in sporting events? Write a short essay expressing your opinion, backing it up with at least three good reasons.

CHAPTER 4: RULERS OF TERABITHIA

Vocabulary: Use the context to determine the meaning of the underlined word in each of the following sentences. Circle the letter of the answer you choose.

1. Jess knew that he was not the best runner in the class, but his <u>consolation</u> was that Gary Fulcher wasn't either.

   a. difficulty   b. comfort   c. enjoyment   d. love

2. When Mrs. Myers' smile shifted suddenly and <u>ominously</u> into a scowl, the class became silent immediately.

   a. calmly   b. lovingly   c. dangerously   d. sweetly

3. Once they were settled into Terabithia, Jess and Leslie knew that no enemy, nor any of the <u>foes</u> whom Leslie imagined attacking Terabithia, could ever defeat them.

   a. cousins   b. families   c. friends   d. enemies

4. After Jess met Leslie, he felt that it was the beginning of a new season in his life, and he chose <u>deliberately</u> to make it so.

   a. purposefully   b. accidentally   c. inadvertently   d. strangely

> Read to find out how two people with opposite personalities could become good friends.

Questions:

1. Why was Jess no longer looking forward to the race?
2. What did Jess's smile at Leslie in the music room signify? Why was this both a difficult and an important step for Jess?
3. What made Leslie and her family seem odd to people in Lark Creek?
4. What did Leslie's essay about her hobby reveal about her character?

Questions for Discussion:

1. Why do you think Jess and Leslie each needed a secret place like Terabithia?
2. Why do you think Jess and Leslie became such good friends?
3. Do you think Leslie's parents could find the life they are seeking in a place like Lark Creek?
4. Why do you think Jess decided to allow his classmates to know about his friendship with Leslie?

Chapter 4: Rulers of Terabithia (cont.)

Literary Element: Characterization

Use the Venn Diagram below to compare the characters of Jess and Leslie. Write the traits they have in common in the overlapping part of the circles.

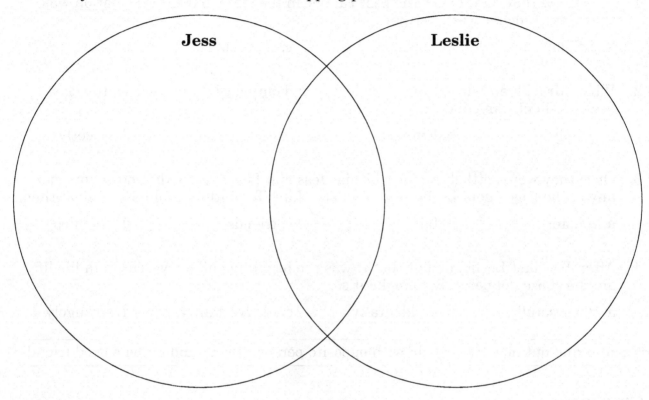

Writing Activity: Dear Diary

Pretend that either Jess or Leslie kept a diary of daily activities. Write a diary entry for one of them telling about a day at Terabithia. Discuss the things you did, what you talked about, and what your feelings were at that time.

CHAPTER 5: THE GIANT KILLERS

Vocabulary: Synonyms are words with similar meanings. Draw a line from each word in column A to its synonym in column B. Then use the words in column A to fill in the blanks in the sentences below.

	A		B
1.	solemn	a.	red
2.	suspend	b.	deny
3.	reject	c.	dove
4.	plunged	d.	cease
5.	crimson	e.	serious

. . . .

1. The hawk _____ from the air to catch the mouse running across the field.

2. Can you _____ payment to the landlord if he does not fix the heating system?

3. I expect the class to _____ your idea that we have additional homework over the weekend.

4. With a _____ expression on his face, the jury foreman pronounced the man guilty.

5. The little girl dressed up in her mother's gown and applied _____ lipstick and powder to her face.

> Read to find out how Jess and Leslie got even.

Questions:

1. Why didn't Leslie want Jess to fight Janice Avery? Why did she think the letter would be a better way to get even.

2. What immediate evidence did Jess and Leslie have that Janice believed the contents of the letter?

3. Why did Jess compare his feelings toward Janice Avery to Leslie's feelings about killer whales?

4. Why was this chapter called "The Giant Killers"?

Chapter 5: The Giant Killers (cont.)

Questions for Discussion:

1. Which kind of punishment do you think is worse — to be beaten up or to be shamed in front of your friends?

2. Do you think Janice deserved the punishment she received?

Writing Activity:

Write about a time when you got even with someone. Tell what made you angry and how you planned your revenge. If this has never happened to you, make up an incident and tell how you would want to get even.

CHAPTER 6: THE COMING OF PRINCE TERRIEN

Vocabulary: Draw a line from each word on the left to its definition on the right. Then use the numbered words to fill in the blanks in the sentences below.

	A		B
1.	obsessed	a.	excess
2.	speculation	b.	abandoned infant
3.	surplus	c.	guess
4.	foundling	d.	clown; fool
5.	jester	e.	preoccupied by one thought

. . . .

1. It is scientific _____ that birds are descended from dinosaurs.

2. The _____ was taken to a nearby hospital after being discovered on the church steps.

3. The king called his _____ to the throne room to entertain his guests.

4. The restaurant sent its _____ food to a homeless shelter.

5. _____ with winning the race, the girl neglected her friends and her schoolwork.

> Read to find out how a prince came into Jess's life.

Questions:

1. Why did Jess fantasize that he was a foundling?

2. Why did Jess find it difficult to think of an appropriate Christmas gift for Leslie?

3. Who was Prince Terrien? Why was this a good gift?

4. Contrast what Jess received for Christmas from Leslie and what he received from his father. Which gift was more appropriate? Why?

Question for Discussion:

Why were the gifts that Jess and Leslie exchanged perfect for one another?

Writing Activity:

Write about a time when you received the perfect gift. If you haven't received one yet, write about an imaginary time. Tell what you want, why you want it, and how this gift might change your life.

CHAPTER 7: THE GOLDEN ROOM

Vocabulary: Antonyms are words with opposite meanings. Draw a line from each word in column A to its antonym in column B. Then use the words in column A to fill in the blanks in the sentences below.

A	B
1. reluctant	a. friendly
2. exiled	b. normal
3. garish	c. misunderstand
4. anxiety	d. eager
5. hostile	e. tasteful
6. comprehend	f. returned
7. weird	g. calmness

. . . .

1. The _____ sound of the wind whistling through the chimney made us tremble.

2. With a change in government, the _____ politicians were allowed to return to their country.

3. His state of _____ increased when the airplane took a rapid nose-dive.

4. It is difficult for me to _____ advanced mathematics.

5. The mother was _____ to allow her twelve-year-old son to travel to the big city alone.

6. The old vaudeville theater was decorated in a(n) _____ style.

7. The United Nations tried to draw up a peace treaty between the two _____ nations.

> Read to find out whether Terabithia would remain a secret.

Questions:

1. Compare and contrast Leslie's relationship with her father with Jess's relationship with his father.

2. What did Jess mean when he said that the Burkes were smart in a way he had never known real live people to be?

3. What was the "sacred place"? What was its significance to Jess and Leslie?

4. What unwritten code of behavior did Janice break? How did Leslie console her and what advice did she offer?

5. How did Jess react when May Belle told him she knew where he went with Leslie? Why did he react this way?

Chapter 7: The Golden Room (cont.)

Questions for Discussion:

Do you think family problems should be discussed publicly, or do you agree with Lark Creek standards that all family matters should remain private? What would happen if someone in your school reported a case of child beating?

Language Study:

Here are two ways to say the same thing. Which one is more expressive? Why do you think Katherine Paterson used the second one?

1. They were very excited when they found a fireplace behind the wall boards.

2. 'They ripped out the boards, coming upon the rusty bricks like prospectors upon the mother lode."

_____

_____

Find a characteristic example of Terabithian language. What kind of language does it imitate?

_____

_____

_____

Writing Activity:

Imagine you are Jess and write a journal entry describing the events in Chapter Seven and your reactions to them. Also, tell how you think things might change now that May Belle knows about Terabithia.

CHAPTER 8: EASTER

Vocabulary: Read the following passage. Then use the context to draw a line from the words on the left to their meanings on the right.

Leslie, who had never attended church before, was excited about the prospect. Jess, on the other hand, sat in his <u>pew</u>, <u>complacent</u> about all that went on around him. As the <u>sanctuary</u> filled with people, he began to daydream and his body and mind became <u>numb</u>. It was not until the <u>congregation</u> began singing in <u>unison</u> and Leslie poked him in the ribs that Jess was roused to attention.

1.	pew	a.	assembly of persons together for religious worship
2.	complacent	b.	lacking emotion or feeling
3.	sanctuary	c.	bench in a church
4.	numb	d.	church or other sacred place
5.	congregation	e.	unbothered; untroubled
6.	unison	f.	producing the same sound at the same time

> Read to find out how church became a problem for Jess's Family

Questions:

1. Why did Easter Sunday become a problem for Jess's family?

2. Why did Jess's mother hesitate about taking Leslie to church? What was her main concern about her own family's appearance that day?

3. Why did Leslie want to go to church?

4. What were Leslie's opinions about the Bible? How did this set her apart even more from the other people in Lark Creek? How was Jess affected by her opinions?

Literary Device: Simile

Find the description of Brenda and Ellie as they appeared on their way to church. Write the simile that is part of that description on the lines below:

_____

_____

What is being compared and what is the effect of this comparison?

_____

Writing Activity:

Write about the relationship between Leslie and Jess — how it began and how it developed and changed.

CHAPTERS 9, 10: THE EVIL SPELL, THE PERFECT DAY

Vocabulary: Synonyms are words with similar meanings; antonyms are words with opposite meanings. In each word group, underline the synonym and circle the antonym for each boldfaced word. Then use the boldfaced words to fill in the blanks in the sentences below.

1. **mournfully**	hopefully	jokingly	joyously	gloomily
2. **emerge**	rise	travel	submerge	swim
3. **sodden**	dried	soaked	shrunken	torn
4. **sporadic**	drenching	occasional	continuous	heavy
5. **vanquished**	conquered	victorious	exhausted	energetic
6. **scrawny**	gentle	thin	plump	trustworthy

. . . .

1. The _____ soldiers were marched before the jubilant general before being sent to labor camps.

2. I couldn't wait to take off my _____ jacket after walking home in the pouring rain.

3. After a lengthy illness, the child seemed weak and _____.

4. The family gazed _____ at the charred remains of what had once been their home.

5. Because they only forecast _____ rain, we did not know whether to carry an umbrella and raincoat.

6. If you look out at sea, you will notice the dolphins _____ from the water for air.

> Read to learn what happened when Jess went to Washington.

Questions:

1. What did Judy mean when she said, "I'm stuck"?

2. Why did Jess and Leslie visit Terabithia even though the weather was bad?

3. Why wouldn't Jess tell Leslie that he would not go to Terabithia?

4. Why didn't Jess ask Miss Edmunds if Leslie could go along with them to Washington?

5. Why did Miss Edmunds take Jess to the National Gallery?

Chapters 9, 10: The Evil Spell, The Perfect Day (cont.)

6. Why was this visit a special treat to Jess?

7. How did Jess know something was wrong when he returned from Washington? Why was his family upset?

Questions for Discussion:

1. In what ways was Leslie the dreamer and Jess the realist? Find specific examples in Chapter Nine. Do you think you are more of a dreamer or a realist?

2. Jess thought that he was a coward and that Leslie was brave. Do you agree with Jess that cowardice is bad and bravery is to be admired? Explain. Are you more like Jess or Leslie?

3. Do you think Jess is guilty in any way for Leslie's death?

Literary Devices:

I. *Personification* — Personification in literature is a device in which an author grants human qualities to non-human objects, animals, or ideas. Find how "dread" is personified in the middle of Chapter Nine as Leslie and Jess stand under the pines. Write this example on the lines below.

_____

_____

What mood do these words create?

_____

II. *Simile* — Find the simile toward the beginning of Chapter Nine in which P.T. is described as he runs ahead of the children toward Terabithia. Write this example on the lines below.

_____

_____

What is being compared?

_____

What mood does this create?

_____

III. *Foreshadowing* — Foreshadowing refers to clues the author provides to predict events that will happen in the novel. Find at least two ways that Leslie's death was foreshadowed in Chapters Nine and Ten.

_____

_____

Chapters 9, 10: The Evil Spell, The Perfect Day (cont.)

Social Studies Connection:

Find an article and pictures of Washington, D.C. in a social studies book, an encyclopedia, or on the internet. Read about and find pictures of all the places Jess saw — the White House, the Washington Monument, the Lincoln and Jefferson Memorials, the Capitol, and all the buildings of the Smithsonian Institute.

Writing Activity:

Write about a time when you felt great happiness and sadness almost at once, as Jess had experienced. Describe what happened and how your feelings changed.

CHAPTERS 11, 12: NO!, STRANDED

Vocabulary: Substitute the underlined word in each sentence below with a more descriptive word from the Word Box. Write the word you choose on the line below the sentence.

┌───┐
│   │
│   │
│   │
└───┘

1. The car <u>turned</u> to the right to avoid a head-on collision with an oncoming truck.

   _____

2. The lawyer tried to <u>dig</u> up secrets about the defendant's past as he questioned him before trial.

   _____

3. The excited puppy <u>jumped</u> into his master's arms after a week-long separation.

   _____

4. In a fit of anger, she <u>threw</u> all the old letters and photographs into the garbage.

   _____

5. <u>Water</u> this plant before you leave for your vacation.

   _____

┌───┐
│   Read to find out how Jess reacted to tragedy.   │
└───┘

Questions:

1. Why do you think Jess denied Leslie's death when he first heard the news?
2. Why did Jess imagine himself apologizing to Leslie for not including her in the trip to Washington?
3. How did Jess's parents show Jess that they loved him and had sympathy for him?
4. How did Jess react when he saw Leslie's grandmother and Bill in tears?
5. Why was Jess angry that Leslie had been cremated?
6. Why did Jess compare himself to an astronaut wandering about on the moon?
7. Why did the Burkes give P.T. to Jess? Why did Jess's parents allow him to have a dog for the first time?
8. At what point did Jess's numbness end? What emotions took its place?

Chapters 11, 12: No!, Stranded (cont.)

Questions for Discussion:

1. Do you think that Jess's reaction to the death of his best friend was normal? Why do you think he didn't cry at Leslie's house?

2. Why do you think Jess threw the paints and drawing paper into the water?

3. Did Leslie's death surprise or disappoint you? Would it have been plausible for the author to have had Jess die instead? Explain your answer.

Writing Activity:

Chapter Eleven was entitled "No!" which represented Jess's strong denial of Leslie's death. Write about a time in your own life or in the life of someone you know that could also be entitled "No!"

CHAPTER 13: BUILDING THE BRIDGE

Vocabulary: Draw a line from each word on the left to its definition on the right. Then use the numbered words to fill in the blanks in the sentences below.

1. traitorous   a. state of utter confusion; turmoil

2. fragile   b. tightness or inward pressure

3. chaos   c. delicate; easily broken

4. constriction   d. disloyal

5. procession   e. act of moving along in an orderly manner

. . . .

1. We packed the _____ crystal bowl in layers of cotton so that it would not break in the mail.

2. My house and all the houses nearby were in a state of _____ after a tornado ripped its way down our block.

3. He felt _____ when he thought about going to the movies without his best friend.

4. The _____ of dignitaries made their way up Fifth Avenue, waving to the crowds along their route.

5. Whenever I eat seafood, I experience a dangerous _____ in my nose and throat, causing me to gasp for breath.

Read to learn how life went forward for Jess

Questions:

1. Why did Jess want to return to his milking chores? What did this reveal about his state of mind?

2. What did Jess do when he returned to Terabithia? Why?

3. In what ways did Leslie still have a strong influence on Jess?

4. How did Mrs. Myers surprise Jess on the day he returned to school?

5. Why did the Burkes take P.T. back? Do you think this was unkind?

Questions for Discussion:

1. After Leslie's death, Jess gained new insights into the character of his father and Mrs. Myers. Are there any adults in your life who you may have misjudged? Would it take a tragedy to see these people in a more favorable light?

2. Why do you think Jess built a bridge to Terabithia and made May Belle the new Queen? Do you think he was being true or disloyal to Leslie?

Chapter 13: Building the Bridge (cont.)

Literary Device: Simile

Locate the simile toward the beginning of Chapter Thirteen in which the author described Jess's growing feelings of peace and acceptance. Write the simile on the lines below.

_____

_____

What was this feeling of peace being compared to?

_____

Do you think this was an apt comparison?

_____

Write a simile of your own to describe a continuing feeling of chaos.

_____

_____

Writing Activity:

Consult a dictionary to find the many meanings of the word "bridge." Then apply several of these definitions to tell why the final chapter was called "Building the Bridge."

CLOZE ACTIVITY

The following excerpt is taken from Chapter Thirteen of the novel. Read it through completely and then go back and fill in the blank spaces with words that make sense. When you have finished, you may compare your language with that of the author.

Jess thought about it all day, how before Leslie came, he had been a nothing — a stupid, weird little kid who drew funny pictures and chased around a cow field trying to act big — trying to hide a whole mob of foolish little fears running riot inside his gut.

It was Leslie who had taken _____[1] from the cow pasture into Terabithia _____[2] turned him into a king. He _____[3] thought that was it. Wasn't king _____[4] best you could be? Now it _____[5] to him that perhaps Terabithia was _____[6] a castle where you came to _____[7] knighted. After you stayed for a _____[8] and grew strong you had to _____[9] on. For hadn't Leslie, even in _____,[10] tried to push back the walls _____[11] his mind and make him see _____[12] to the shining world — huge and _____[13] and beautiful and very fragile? (Handle _____[14] care — everything — even the predators.)

Now _____[15] was·time for him to move _____.[16] She wasn't there, so he must _____[17] for both of them. It was _____[18] to him to pay back to _____[19] world in beauty and caring what _____[20] had loaned him in vision and _____.[21]

As for the terrors ahead — for _____[22] did not fool himself that they were _____[23] behind him — well, you just have _____[24] stand up to your fear and _____[25] let it squeeze you white. Right, _____?[26]

Right.

POST-READING ACTIVITIES

1. **Readers Theater:** Select one portion of the novel to present to the class. It may be chosen because it conveys an important message, is very moving, is amusing, or contains interesting language. The passage can be read aloud or presented as Readers Theater in which one student reads the narration and other students read the characters' roles.

2. **Art Connetion:** Design a diorama to represent Terabithia using a shoe box as the container. You may utilize paper and found objects for the scenery within.

3. Have you ever experienced the death of a close friend or family member? Was your reaction similar to Jess's: going through stages of rejection, anger, repressed grief, and finally sad resignation? Or did you experience the situation in a different way?

4. Although the author Katherine Paterson has stated that she does not intend to write a sequel to this novel, you may write one yourself. Imagine Jess as a young man and determine the career he might choose. Where do you think he would live? Would there always be a "Terabithia" in his life? Would his friendship with Leslie continue to influence him or would he forget her?

5. Find an obituary written on the occasion of the death of a well-known person that appears in a current newspaper. Notice the kind of information that is included in the article. Then write an obituary commemorating Leslie Burke's life and death. Tell all the facts you know about her and her family and describe her distinctive character traits.

6. **Cooperative Learning Activity:** Leslie introduced Jess to many of the wonderful books she had read and Miss Edmunds introduced Jess to the works of master artists at the National Gallery. Work with a small cooperative learning group to create a list of books and a list of places that someone like Jess would enjoy. In each case, indicate why you think it would be appealing.

7. **Literacy Element-Charaterization:** Consider the changes that occurred in Jess during the course of the novel. Use a Venn diagram such as the one below to compare Jess at the beginning and at the end of the novel. Write the characteristics that did not change in the overlapping part of the circles. Then write a character sketch of Jess.

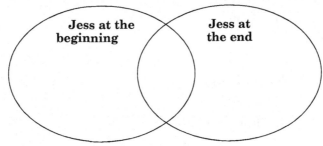

8. *Bridge to Terabithia* won the prestigious Newbery Award which is granted each year to the best book for young people as determined by the American Library Association. Why do you think the award was granted to this book? Do you agree with the choice?

SUGGESTIONS FOR FURTHER READING

* Babbitt, Natalie. *Search for Delicious.* Square Fish.
* _____. *Tuck Everlasting.* Square Fish.
* Bauer, Marion Dane. *On My Honor.* Dell.
* Buyea, Rob. *Because of Mr. Terupt.* Yearling.
  Dixon, Paige. *A Time to Love, A Time to Mourn.* Scholastic.
* Green, John. *The Fault in Our Stars.* Penguin.
* _____. *Turtles All the Way Down.* Dutton.
* Greene, Bette. *Philip Hall likes me, I reckon maybe.* Puffin.
  Greene, Constance C. *Beat the Turtle Drum.* Puffin.
  Hermes, Patricia. *You Shouldn't Have to Say Goodbye.* Scholastic.
* Holman, Felice. *Slake's Limbo.* Aladdin.
* Jukes, Mavis. *Blackberries in the Dark.* Yearling.
* Konigsburg, E.L. *Jennifer, Hecate, Macbeth, William McKinley, and Me, Elizabeth.* Atheneum.
* _____. *The View From Saturday.* Atheneum
* Lewis, C.S. *The Lion, the Witch and the Wardrobe.* HarperCollins.
  Lowry, Lois. *A Summer to Die.* HMH Books.
  Mazer, Norma Fox. *A Figure of Speech.* Laurel Leaf.
* Smith, Doris. *A Taste of Blackberries.* HarperCollins.
* Speare, Elizabeth. *The Witch of Blackbird Pond.* HMH Books.
  Thomas, Marlo. *Free to Be . . . You and Me.* MS. Foundation.

Some Other Books by Katherine Paterson

  Angels and Other Strangers. HarperCollins.
* *Come Sing, Jimmy Jo.* Puffin.
  Flip-Flop Girl. Puffin.
* *The Great Gilly Hopkins.* HarperCollins.
* *Jacob Have I Loved.* HarperCollins.
* *Jip, His Story.* Puffin.
* *Lyddie.* Puffin.
* *The Master Puppeteer.* HarperCollins.
  My Brigadista Year. Candlewick.
  Of Nightingales that Weep. HarperCollins.
* *Park's Quest.* Puffin.
  The Sign of the Chrysanthemum. HarperCollins.

* NOVEL-TIES Study Guides are available for these titles.

ANSWER KEY

Chapter 1

Vocabulary: 1. f 2. d 3. a 4. e 5. c 6. b; 1. stroll 2. obediently 3. despised 4. crouched 5. puny 6. brag

Language
Study: 1. Momma would be very angry. 2. He was a middle child with two older and two younger sisters. 3. He had more courage and endurance than anyone else. 4. He won the whole race, not only one heat.

Background
Information: 1. The story begins during the summer, specifically in August. The Aaron family farm is located in Lark Creek, a suburb of Washington, D.C. The Aaron family consists of ten-year-old Jesse, who is entering fifth grade; his younger sisters, seven-year-old first grader May Belle and four-year-old Joyce Ann; his older sisters, Brenda and Ellie; Momma and Dad, who works in Washington, digging and hauling.

Questions: 1. As the only boy in the family, Jess had to do the chores. Because he liked to draw, his father had little respect for him. 2. Jess took on the challenge of being the fastest runner in fifth grade. Answers to the second part of the question will vary, but should include the ideas that Jess was goal oriented, was competitive, and didn't want to be ostracized any longer for being an artistic boy. 3. Jess was too preoccupied with his perceived unfair treatment at home, the chores that had to be done, and his personal desire to be the best runner in his grade to be concerned with his new neighbors.

Chapter 2

Vocabulary: 1. pandemonium – wild uproar 2. hypocritical – affecting virtues or opinions one does not have 3. scalding – burning 4. anticipation – expectation; advance of 5. endure – tolerate; put up with

Questions: 1. Jess loved to draw so much that it seemed like an addiction. 2. Jess's father scorned his son's drawing, considering it an effeminate pastime. 3. Not only was Miss Edmunds young and beautiful, she appreciated Jess's artwork and seemed to like him as a person. Jess felt that they were both outcasts in the rural backwash of Lark Creek. 4. Jess was disappointed that his new neighbor was a girl. He couldn't imagine establishing a friendship with a girl.

Chapter 3

Vocabulary: 1. g 2. c 3. d 4. e 5. f 6. b 7. a; 1. conspicuous 2. repulsive 3. postponed 4. drought 5. gaze 6. focus 7. retreat

Questions: 1. Leslie's unconventional, casual dress was considered odd by her primly dressed classmates. Leslie didn't care about the opinions of others. 2. On his first day of fifth grade, Jess determined that he did not like his teacher and he was annoyed by Gary Fulcher's taunting. 3. Jess didn't care about Leslie or about women's rights. He just wanted to challenge Gary Fulcher.

Chapter 4

Vocabulary: 1. b 2. c 3. d 4. a

Questions: 1. Jess was no longer looking forward to the race because, although he would be able to beat Gary Fulcher, he knew he could not beat Leslie. 2. The smile indicated that Jess recognized Leslie as a friend. By accepting the friendship of a girl who was considered odd by Lark Creek standards, Jess, for the first time, was willing to stand up to peer pressure and become more self-confident. 3. Leslie and her family seemed odd because they came from the city, had money, were intellectuals, and didn't have a TV. 4. Leslie's scuba diving hobby indicated that she was adventurous, a risk taker, and very athletic.

Chapter 5

Vocabulary: 1. e 2. d 3. b 4. c 5. a; 1. plunged 2. suspend 3. reject 4. solemn 5. crimson

Questions: 1. Leslie didn't want Jess to fight Janice Avery because she didn't think that was the best way to get revenge, and she didn't want Jess to be beaten up in return. Leslie realized that the letter, which would cause Janice to be humiliated, was a more exquisite form of punishment. 2. It was clear that Janice believed the contents of the letter because right after school Jess and Leslie could see Janice in a huddle with her friends, presumably boasting about the letter. 3. Like killer whales, who were dangerous animals, Janice might need protection. 4. Janice was the giant and Jess and Leslie were the giant killers.

Chapter 6

Vocabulary: 1. e 2. c 3. a 4. b 5. d; 1. speculation 2. foundling 3. jester 4. surplus 5. obsessed

Questions: 1. Jeff fantasized that he was a foundling because he felt alienated from his sisters and his family. He felt that his father was not proud of him and that he could never please him. 2. It was hard to find the perfect gift for Leslie - one that would show that he cared for her. He wanted to be proud of the gift. 3. Prince Terrien was the name of the puppy that Jess gave Leslie. This was a good gift because it made Leslie happy; it was something she wouldn't have bought for herself; and it was fun. 4. Leslie's gift was a box of watercolors, three brushes, and a pad of heavy art paper. His father's gift was a set of electric trains which were hard to operate. Jess loved Leslie's gift because it was something he wanted and would use for his special drawings. Leslie knew Jess so well that she understood what he wanted; his father didn't appreciate Jess's preferences and therefore gave him an inappropriate present.

Chapter 7

Vocabulary: 1. d 2. f 3. e 4. g 5. a 6. c 7. b; 1. weird 2. exiled 3. anxiety 4. comprehend 5. reluctant 6. garish 7. hostile

Questions: 1. Leslie had a warm and close relationship with her father based on mutual trust and need. Jess had no feelings of warmth toward his father and felt that he could never please him. 2. Jess meant that the Burkes were college-educated and knowledgeable about music, art, and literature. People Jess knew had common sense, knowledge, and practical values. 3. The pine grove was the "sacred place." It was important because it was a secret place where Jess and Leslie could be true to themselves, a place where no one would intrude on their lives. 4. Kids protected their parents' reputations; Janice had betrayed her father by telling her friends that he beat her. Leslie told Janice how she had been teased; she advised her to pretend that she didn't know what her tormentors were talking about. 5. Jess was furious that May Belle knew about his secret place. He worried that she would tell his mother who would tease him and forbid him to go to Terabithia. He was also angry that the place was no longer a secret.

Chapter 8

Vocabulary: 1. c 2. e 3. d 4. b 5. a 6. f

Questions: 1. Easter Sunday was a problem for Jess's family because Jess's father was laid off and the girls could not afford to buy new outfits. They balked about going to church dressed in their old clothes. 2. Jess's mother was reluctant to take Leslie to church because she was afraid Leslie would not wear a dress. She knew that Leslie's family had more money and education than she did and she did not want Leslie sneering at her. She wanted her family to have new clothes. 3. Leslie wanted to go to church because she thought it would be a new and interesting experience. 4. Leslie thought the Bible was a beautiful and interesting story. She didn't believe in being damned to hell as the rest of the people in Lark Creek believed. She caused Jess to begin to question some of his own beliefs.

Chapter 9, 10

Vocabulary: 1. mournfully: S – gloomily, A – joyously 2. emerge: S – rise, A – submerge 3. sodden: S – soaked, A – dried 4. sporadic: S – occasional, A – continuous 5. vanquished: S – conquered, A – victorious 6. scrawny: S – thin, A – plump; 1. vanquished 2. sodde 3. scrawny 4. mournfully 5. sporadic 6. emerge

Questions: 1. When Judy said she was stuck she meant she had writer's block, a time when she couldn't think of anything to write. 2. Leslie and Jess visited Terabithia because they were bored and had nothing else to do. 3. Jess didn't tell Leslie that he would not go to Terabithia because he didn't want her to know that he was afraid; in fact, he didn't want to be afraid. 4. Jess didn't ask Miss Edmunds to take Leslie along because he didn't think of it in the rush to go, and then he was happy to be alone with Miss Edmunds. 5. Miss Edmunds took Jess to the National Gallery because she knew that he loved to draw and suspected that he had never been there. 6. Jess enjoyed seeing the pictures in the gallery, enjoying their color and form and hugeness. Jess had never seen real paintings, but he had dreamed of becoming an artist himself. 7. Jess saw his father's truck at home unusually early in the day and his family gathered together not even watching television. They were upset because of Leslie's death and they thought Jess might have died, too. Obviously, Jess's mother did not recall Jess's request to go to Washington while she was still drowsy.

Chapter 11, 12

Vocabulary: 1. swerved 2. dredge 3. leaped 4. flung 5. douse

Questions: 1. Answers to this question will vary, but should include the idea that it is normal for people to deny tragedy even in the face of its inevitability. 2. The apology was an expression of his feelings of guilt. In his imagination he concluded that Leslie would still be alive if he had invited her to come along to Washington. 3. Jess's father did the milking chores, his mother made him a special breakfast, and stopped the older girls from taunting him. His father offered him physical affection as consolation for his anger. 4. Jess was embarrassed to see adults crying. 5. Jess felt resentful about Leslie's cremation because he couldn't see Leslie for one last time and no one had consulted him. 6. Jess felt abandoned and lonely like an astronaut on the moon. 7. The Burkes gave P.T. to Jess because they were going to Pennsylvania and needed someone to take care of their dog. Jess's parents allowed their son to have the dog because it would provide him some comfort, since it was the only remaining link to his friend Leslie. 8. Jess began to react emotionally to the tragedy by throwing away the paints, Leslie's gift to him. His reactions ran the gamut from hatred and anger, to sadness, and finally acceptance.

Chapter 13

Vocabulary: 1. d 2. c 3. a 4. b 5. e; 1. fragile 2. chaos 3. traitorous 4. procession 5. constriction

Questions: 1. Jess wanted to milk the cows early so that he could feel life was returning to normal. This suggests that Jess was getting ready to get on with his life. 2. When Jess returned to Terabithia, he made a funeral wreath and went with P.T. in a procession to the sacred grove and then to the castle. Answers to the second part of the question will vary, but should include the idea that Jess was paying homage to Leslie. 3. Jess adopted Leslie's language and her attitude when he offered his tribute to her at Terabithia. He helped May Belle overcome her fear the way Leslie helped Janice Avery. 4. Jess, who had always assumed Mrs. Myers to be a heartless woman, was astonished by her deep feelings for Leslie and her sympathy for him. 5. The Burkes took back P.T. because the dog was a living reminder of Leslie. Answers to second part of the question will vary.